better together*

*This book is best read together, grownup and kid.

 akidsco.com

a
kids
book
about

a kids book about

dyslexia

by Sarah Travers

A Kids Co.
Editor Emma Wolf
Designer Rick DeLucco
Creative Director Rick DeLucco
Studio Manager Kenya Feldes
Sales Director Melanie Wilkins
Head of Books Jennifer Goldstein
CEO and Founder Jelani Memory

DK
Delhi Technical Team Bimlesh Tiwary Pushpak Tyagi, Rakesh Kumar
Senior Production Editor Jennifer Murray
Senior Production Controller Louise Minihane
Senior Acquisitions Editor Katy Flint
Acquisitions Project Editor Sara Forster
Managing Art Editor Vicky Short
Managing Director, Licensing Mark Searle

First American edition, 2025
Published in the United States by DK Publishing, 1745 Broadway, 20th Floor,
New York, NY 10019

First published in Great Britain in 2025 by
Dorling Kindersley Limited, 20 Vauxhall Bridge Road, London SW1V 2SA
A Penguin Random House Company

The authorised representative in the EEA is
Dorling Kindersley Verlag GmbH. Arnulfstr. 124, 80636 Munich, Germany

A catalog record for this book is available from the Library of Congress.
A CIP catalogue record for this book is available from the British Library.
ISBN: 978-0-2417-4380-5

DK books are available at special discounts when purchased in bulk for sales
promotions, premiums, fund-raising, or education use. For details, contact:
DK Publishing Special Markets, 1745 Broadway, 20th Floor, New York, NY 10019
SpecialSales@dk.com

Printed and bound in China
www.dk.com
akidsco.com

MIX
Paper | Supporting
responsible forestry
FSC™ C018179

This book was made with Forest
Stewardship Council™ certified
paper – one small step in DK's
commitment to a sustainable future.
**Learn more at www.dk.com/uk/
information/sustainability**

To my mom, who taught
me to stand up for myself.

To my dad, who always told
me to follow my heart.

To my husband, who
always believes in me.

To my girls: remember
to think outside the box.
It's beautiful out here.

Intro
for grownups

Did school feel hard for you growing up? As a parent or caregiver, do you notice your kid struggling in school? When our kids are facing challenges in their day-to-day lives, it can be scary and frustrating as a grownup who cares for them to not always know exactly how to help.

Growing up with dyslexia myself, it felt like I had to work so much harder than my peers in order to just get by in school. I had to learn how to advocate for myself and find the support I needed to learn and grow.

Someone with dyslexia might need you to rephrase a question or explain something in a different way. My favorite teachers were the ones who took the time to connect with me, remind me that I am smart, and find creative ways to support my learning.

I wrote this book to help you and your kid feel seen, heard, supported, and empowered. You have a smart kid with a beautiful brain that will take them to amazing places!

Hi! My name is Sarah.

And this is a book about

Dyslexia is a lea

rning disability.

It makes

reading,

writing,

and

spelling

hard.

People with dyslexia think about things differently.

Sometimes, dyslexia is described as trying to read while looking in a mirror.

Sometimes, dyslexia is described as trying to read while looking in a mirror.

b d

For some people, the letters "b" and "d"

d b

p q

get flipped, as well as "p" and "q."

q p

For example, think of the word

"house

For me, I read that as

"house

boat."

poat."

But, I know there's no such thing as a housepoat (or housedoat, or houseqoat—other common ways to read that word).

In order to read that word correctly, I process through each of these options and eliminate the ones which don't make sense.

I get to the same answer as anyone else, but I have to go through way more steps to get there.

Does this sound familiar to you?

Do you or does someone you know process things in a similar way?

The first thing I want you
to know is people with dyslexia are ● ● ●

so smart.

That multi-step process their brain works through is something that happens all day long, every single day.

That takes so much work!
And it can be exhausting.

Another thing I want you to know is that not all people need to do their work in the same way.

I've learned a lot about this through my own experience with dyslexia.

Two key components for finding what works best are **patience and adaptability.**

Every person can thrive when met with patience and care in their learning experience.

For people with dyslexia, this is especially important for their success.

Grownups,

be patient with the kids in your life who have different needs.

Be willing to take breaks and move more slowly when needed.

Kids,

be patient with yourselves.

You are working really hard.

You will learn what you need to.

You are not behind—you are
right on your own schedule.

And if learning one way
isn't working for you...

try something

new!

(That's the adaptability piece.)

Learning isn't a one-size-fits-all thing, and different brains need different things.

For example...

- My mom used to trace the shape of letters on my back, so I could feel what they looked like.

- You can use different colors (pens, notecards) to remember specific definitions and categories of things.

- It helps me to hear and read something at the same time.

- Read a book upside down!

- Have discussions in groups to learn from others' perspectives.

- Ask "why" over and over until you hear it in a way that works for you.

- If someone extends an opportunity for help, take it!

Any strategy that works best for you **is awesome.**

And if you need something different than what's offered, it's important to ask for it.

When I was in college, I had a reader with me for tests.

They would literally read each word of a question, and I could answer as I heard the words spoken aloud.

They wouldn't answer the questions for me (in fact, they sometimes pronounced words wrong!), but it helps my brain to hear things out loud.

If you feel like you need a different learning strategy in school, what can you do?

First of all, being tested for dyslexia is a great place to start.

It's very important that you and your grownups speak up for what you need with your teachers and the principal of your school.

And it can take a while to get the tests approved.

Once you do, the tests can be long (like, several days), but it's totally worth it.

Your results for the test include a list of possible accommodations to help you in the classroom.

And with that list in hand, I encourage you to meet with your teachers and ask them how they can help you get what you need out of school.

This might sound scary.
And complicated.
And also unfair.

You might be thinking,
why don't all kids
take a test like this?

But you are

You are

And you

brave.

capable.

can do this.

Learning how to advocate for yourself is something everyone needs to do.

You're just learning how to do it way earlier, and this will serve you for the rest of your life.

And, guess what?

You're not alone.

Who are the people
in your life who support
you and believe in you?

Who takes the time to
make sure you understand
what's happening?

A parent?

A teacher?

A classmate

or friend?

Let your personal connections empower you and fuel your determination in learning.

You have the power to chart your path.

One more thing I want you to know—
the way you think about and see
the world is beautiful.

I love my brain because it helps me
be a good problem-solver, allows
me to see the big picture, and
increases my empathy for others.

Embrace your unique creativity and the ways in which *you* think outside the box.

You are super cool, exactly as you are.

My mom always told me it takes many colors to make a rainbow.

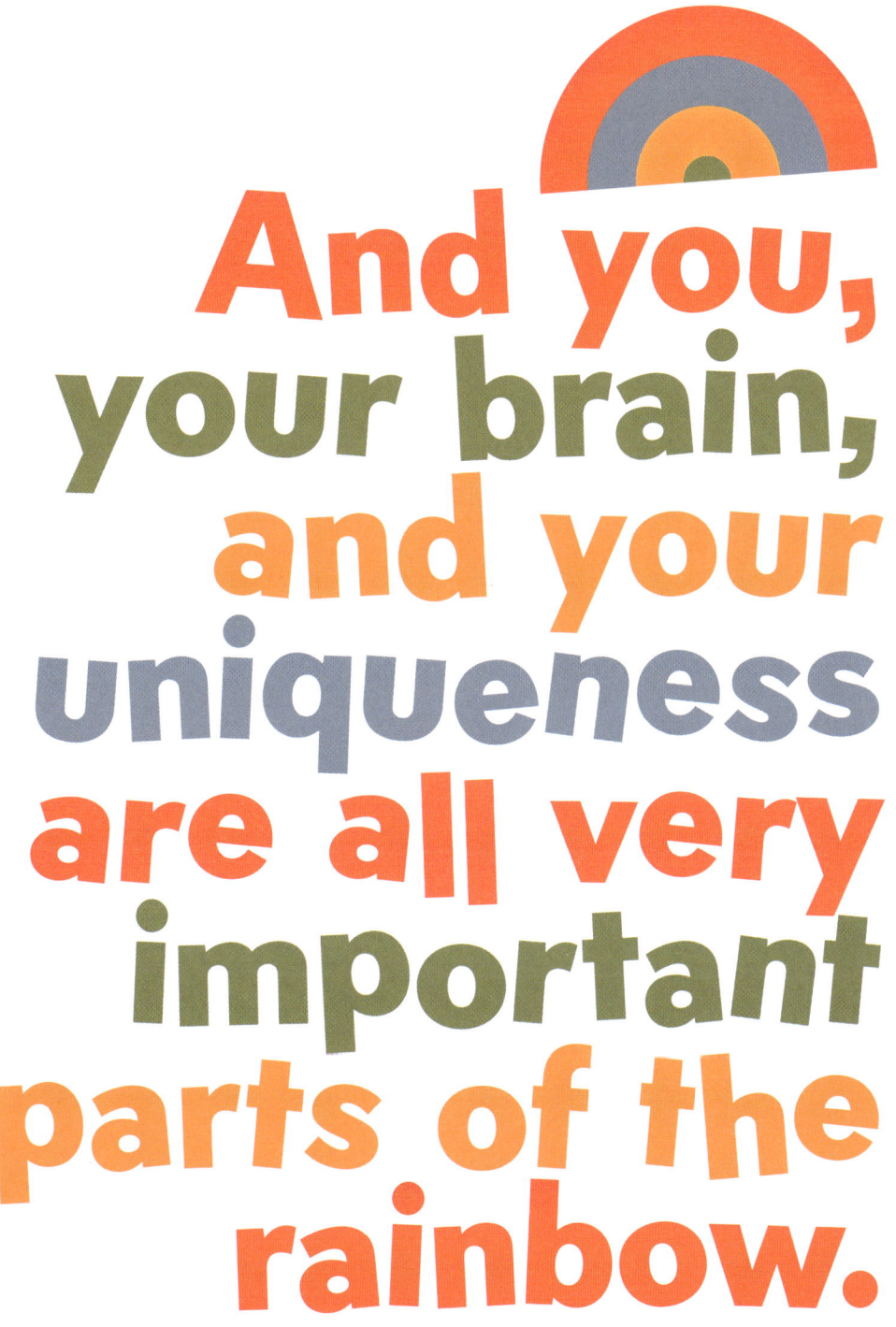

And you, your brain, and your uniqueness are all very important parts of the rainbow.

Outro
for grownups

What can you do from here? I'm glad you asked! Take time to slow down, connect with the kid(s) in your life with dyslexia, and try to work through problems from their perspective. Think outside the box and focus on how they connect with new material and what might help take away some of the pressure of school.

Help them discover passions they can be challenged by and succeed in outside of the classroom to build confidence.

Remind them they are smart, even if school is hard.

Make a point to meet with teachers and administrators regularly to share your observations and concerns—they are there to help your kid succeed.

Don't ever feel ashamed about dyslexia. Hold onto these wise words my mom shared with me: Asking for accommodations in school is no different than going to the doctor for eyeglasses when you can't see the board.

About The Author

Sarah Travers (she/her) is a transformational holistic health coach and trauma-informed breathwork facilitator who helps people find their passions and learn to love and trust themselves. She is a mother to 2 wonderful young girls and lives with her family on their organic vegetable farm in rural Maryland.

Sarah was diagnosed with dyslexia in the second grade. She wrote this book to share her experiences and to remind others that, while learning may be challenging, they are exceptional individuals who have lots to contribute in the classroom and beyond.

Growing up with dyslexia can be hard, and kids need to know they are not alone in their journey. They need love and support to build their confidence and learn how to stand up for themselves.

This book is meant to comfort and inspire students and their families. People with dyslexia are smart, strong, and capable of great things!

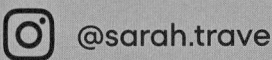 @sarah.travers   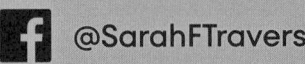 @SarahFTravers   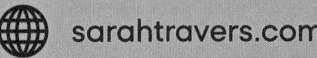 sarahtravers.com

Made to empower.

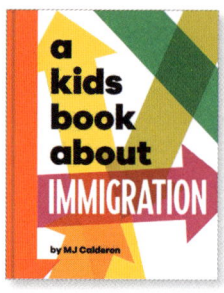

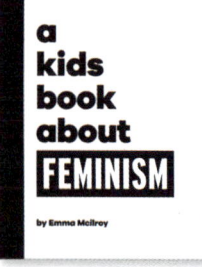

Discover more at akidsco.com